1ST GRADE PHONICS
Unit 10
Spelling Mixed Syllable Types

TABLE OF CONTENTS

IMPORTANT: Please refer to the Teacher Guide for specific scripts, procedures, and words that are represented by pictures.

Throughout this Unit, learners will scan QR codes. Be careful they scan each code individually.

LEARN

- Spelling a variety of syllable types
- Reading a variety of syllable types
- Spelling compound words

DAILY PAGE GOALS

Day	Complete	Day	Complete	Day	Complete
1	ii–6	7	32–38	13	63–68
2	7–13	8	39–45	14	69–75
3	14–20	9	46–51	15	76–81
4	21–25	10	52–56	16	82–87
5	26–27	11	57–58	17	88–89
6	28–31	12	59–62	18	90–93

Teacher reads all pages to the learners.

1. SPELLING LIST 16: Part 1

Learn:

- Identify different syllable types.

- Spell and read words from List 16.

WRITING PHONOGRAM REVIEW

✏️ **Listen to and write the phonograms.**
Underline any multi-letter phonograms.

WORKING WITH WORDS

The words in List 16 have digraph **sh**. They also have different types of syllables.

✏️ **Write the correct answers.**
Write the words by the correct clues.

fish	Shay	shoe
shark	shirt	Josh

1) My home is in the water.

   I am an r-controlled syllable. _____

2) My home is in the water.

   I am a closed syllable. _____

3) You wear me.

   I am a tricky word. _____

4) You wear me.

   I am an r-controlled syllable. _____

5) I am a name.

   I am a vowel team syllable. _____

6) I am a name.

   I am a closed syllable. _____

2

Listen!

Circle the correct answers.

| 7) | syllables | 1 | 2 | 3 | 4 |

| 8) | sounds | 1 | 2 | 3 | 4 |

Write and read.

9) _____

Choose the correct answer.

10) What is the syllable type?
   - ○ vowel team
   - ○ r-controlled
   - ○ open

 **Circle the correct answers.**

| 11) | syllables | 1 | 2 | 3 | 4 |

| 12) | sounds | 1 | 2 | 3 | 4 |

 **Write and read.**

13) _____

 **Choose the correct answers.**

14) Mark (☒) the TWO things that make this word tricky.

☐ It has a silent consonant.

☐ It has a silent final **e**.

☐ The vowel team does not make its usual sounds.

Listen!

? Circle the correct answers.

| 15) | syllables | 1 | 2 | 3 | 4 |

| 16) | sounds | 1 | 2 | 3 | 4 |

✏ Write and read.

17) _____

? Choose the correct answer.

18) What is the syllable type?
- ○ r-controlled
- ○ VCe
- ○ open

 **Choose the correct answer.**

19) Which word has a long vowel sound?

    ◯ shout   ◯ should   ◯ shape

 **Write the correct answers.**
Complete the sentences.

shout	shape	should

20) Shelby heard a loud _____, "It's time to go!"

21) Shelby knew that she _____ be leaving, but she did not want to.

22) She was making a card in the _____ of a star.

SCORE   CORRECT   RESCORE

2. SPELLING LIST 16: Part 2

Learn:

- Divide two-syllable words.

- Spell and read words from List 16.

WRITING PHONOGRAM REVIEW

 **Listen to and write the phonograms.**
Underline any multi-letter phonograms.

WORKING WITH WORDS

Mark, divide, and read the words.
Circle the syllable division pattern. Write each syllable.
Remember, underline the multi-letter phonograms first.

Word	Pattern	Syllable 1	Syllable 2
1) s<u>h</u>amr<u>o</u><u>ck</u> V C C V	VCV (VCCV)	sham	rock
2) furnish	VCV VCCV		
3) shelter	VCV VCCV		
4) skirmish	VCV VCCV		
5) shaggy	VCV VCCV		
6) tarnish	VCV VCCV		

Listen!

Circle the correct answers.

7)	syllables	1	2	3	4

8)	sounds	1	2	3	4

Write and read.

9) _____

Choose the correct answer.

10) Which position is the vowel in?
   - ○ beginning
   - ○ middle
   - ○ ending

 Circle the correct answers.

| 11) | syllables | 1 | 2 | 3 | 4 |

| 12) | sounds | 1 | 2 | 3 | 4 |

 Write and read.

13) _____

 Choose the correct answer.

14) Which spelling rule does this word follow?
- ○ ending **ch** sound
- ○ floss rule
- ○ ending **k** sound

Listen!

Circle the correct answers.

15)

syllables	1	2	3	4

16) | sounds | 1 | 2 | 3 | 4 |
|---|---|---|---|---|

Write and read.

17)

Choose the correct answer.

18) What is the syllable type?
- ○ closed
- ○ VCe
- ○ r-controlled

Listen!

Circle the correct answers.

19) | syllables | 1 | 2 | 3 | 4 |

20) | sounds | 1 | 2 | 3 | 4 |

Write and read.

21) _____

Choose the correct answer.

22) Which spelling rule does this word follow?
- ○ suffix **es**
- ○ short vowel sound
- ○ ending **ch** sound

? Choose the correct answers.

23) Mark (☒) TWO words that have long vowel sounds.

☐ she   ☐ shake   ☐ dish

✏ Write the correct answers.
Sort the words in ABC order.

trash	dish	she

24) _____

25) _____

26) _____

✏ Use the word in your own sentence.

shake

27) _____

SCORE ◯   CORRECT ◯   RESCORE ◯

3. SPELLING LIST 16: Part 3

Learn:

- Read sentences with digraph **sh**.

- Spell and read words from List 16.

WRITING PHONOGRAM REVIEW

Listen to and write the phonograms.
Underline any multi-letter phonograms.

WORKING WITH WORDS

 **Read.**

It was a sunny day in the lush valley of Sheep Town. Shane brushed his coat. Then, he went out to play.

Shane was a shy sheep. If any sheep talked to him, he blushed and hid. He liked to dash from shrub to shrub by himself.

On this sunny day, Shane saw something shiny in a bush. He rushed to get it. It was a silver shield with a red star. "How cool!" Shane shouted.

A group of sheep heard this and ran to see. Shane was so happy, he forgot all about feeling shy. He showed off the shield to his new pals.

 **Choose the correct answers.**

1) What did Shane do before he went out to play?

He brushed his coat.　He watched TV.　He ate breakfast.

2) How did Shane feel after finding the shield?

shy　　　　　　　angry　　　　　　happy

3) What did Shane do when other sheep came to see the shield?
- ○ He hid it.
- ○ He showed it to them.
- ○ He ran away.

16

Listen!

 **Circle the correct answers.**

| 4) | syllables | 1 | 2 | 3 | 4 |

| 5) | sounds | 1 | 2 | 3 | 4 |

 **Write and read.**

6) _____

 **Choose the correct answer.**

7) What is the syllable type?
- ○ vowel team
- ○ closed
- ○ open

Listen!

? **Circle the correct answers.**

8) | syllables | 1   2   3   4

9) | sounds | 1   2   3   4

✏️ **Write and read.**

10) _____

? **Choose the correct answer.**

11) The vowel sound is ____.
   - ○ short
   - ○ long
   - ○ r-controlled

Listen!

 **Circle the correct answers.**

| 12) | syllables | 1 | 2 | 3 | 4 |

| 13) | sounds | 1 | 2 | 3 | 4 |

 **Write and read.**

14) _____

 **Choose the correct answer.**

15) What is the syllable type?
- ○ VCe
- ○ open
- ○ r-controlled

 **Choose the correct answers.**

16) Mark (☒) TWO words that have short vowel sounds.

☐ shine ☐ shut ☐ shop

 **Circle the correct answers.**
Which picture describes the sentence?

17) The gate stays **shut** to keep the baby safe.

18) The boy walked into the **shop**.

19) The cars **shine** in the sunlight.

SCORE CORRECT RESCORE

PHONOGRAM REVIEW

 Listen to and circle the correct phonograms.

1)    au   aw   ou

2)    ow   wh   u

3)    ey   ee   ea

4)    oo   o   a

5)    l   h   wh

6) sh   tch   ch

7) ue   u   oe

8) ar   ear   r

9) h   kn   l

10) ph   b   f

11) s   c   wr

12) ough   a   y

13) i   igh   ci

14) nk   p   qu

15) x   wh   th

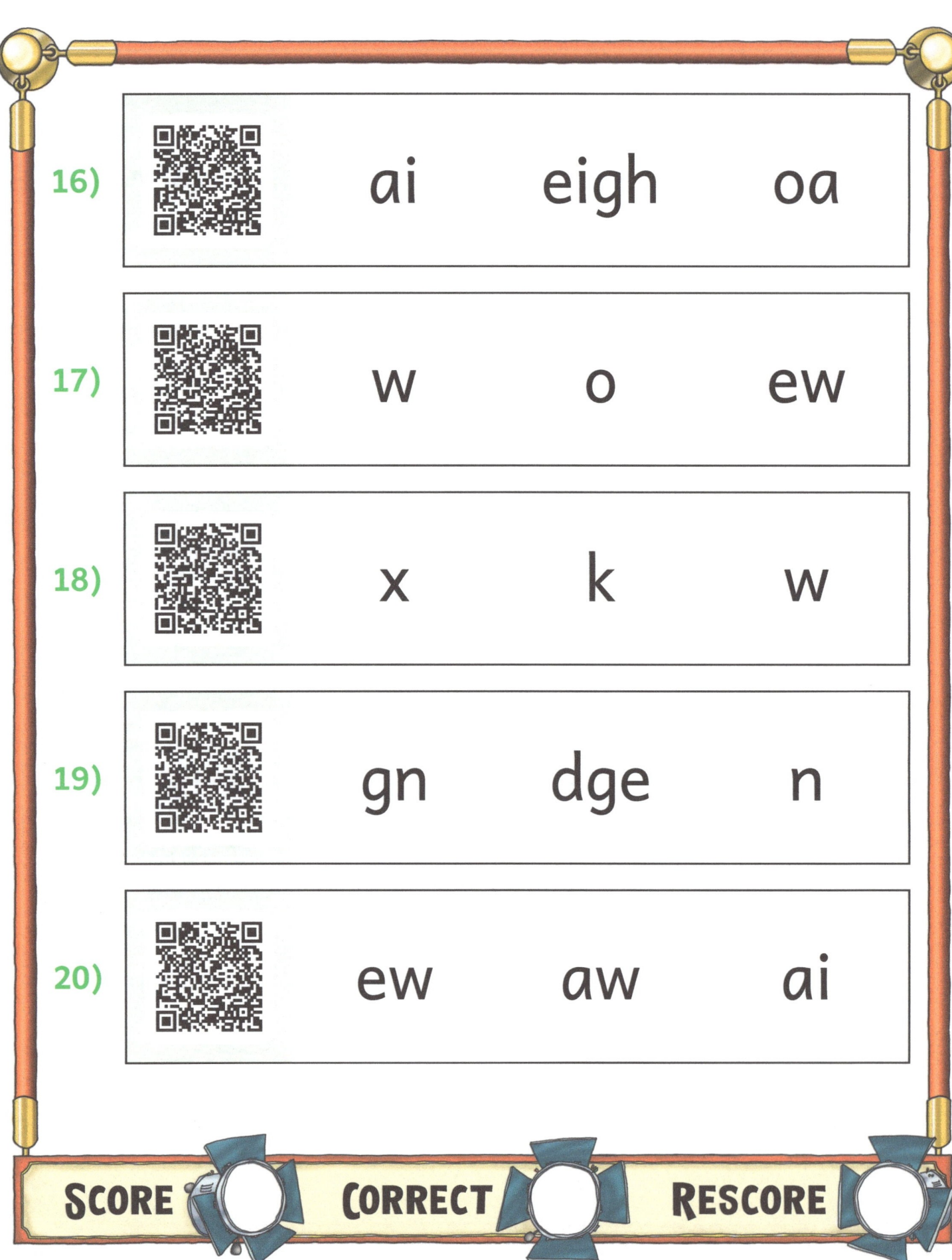

16) ai eigh oa

17) w o ew

18) x k w

19) gn dge n

20) ew aw ai

SCORE CORRECT RESCORE

 **Write the correct answers.**
Write the words in the boxes.

should   trash   shut   shout   shop

1)

2)

3)

4)

5)

shake   she   shine   shape   dish

6)

7)

8)

9)

10)

This Reader has the tricky word *ocean*. The letters **ce** make the **sh** sound. This only happens in a few other words.

Tricky Word
ocean

Write the correct answers.
Complete the sentences.

shell	sharp	ship

1) We can sail the ocean on a _____.

2) I found this _____ on the ocean shore.

3) Sharks in the ocean have _____ teeth.

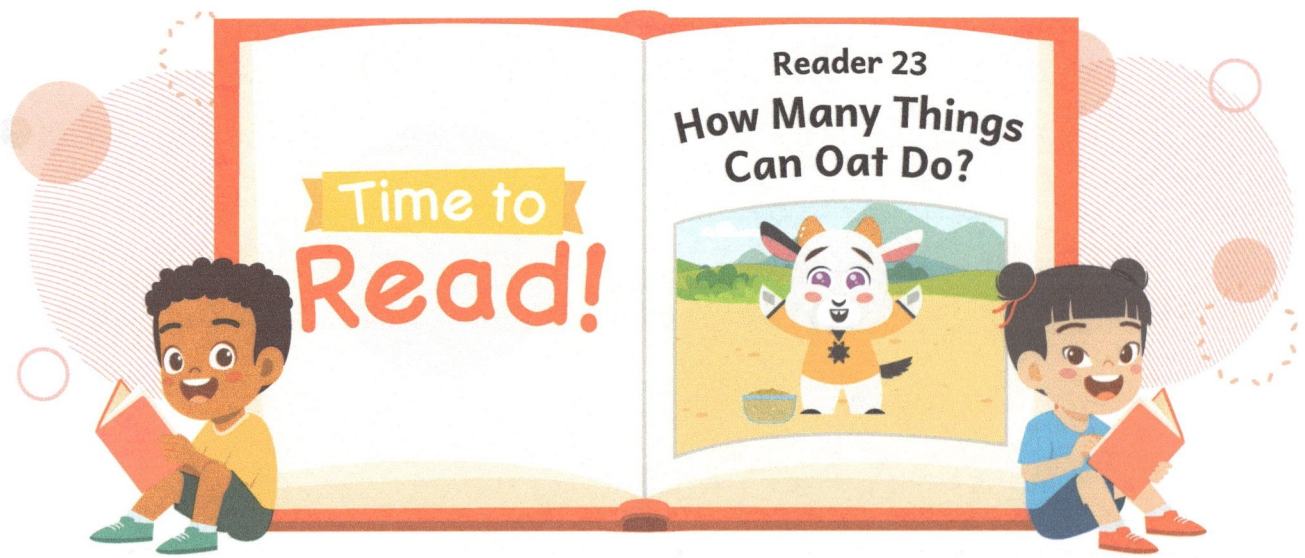

Time to **Read!**

Reader 23
How Many Things Can Oat Do?

 **Choose the correct answers.**

4) What did Tug want to know?
- ○ how many things Oat can do
- ○ how to surf in the ocean
- ○ how to sail a boat

5) What was the first thing Oat did?
- ○ set up a shop
- ○ run up a sand hill
- ○ land on a boat

6) What was the last thing Oat did?
- ○ serve milk to his pals
- ○ jump into the air
- ○ surf to the beach

Phonogram Test 28

Listen to and write the correct phonograms.
Underline any multi-letter phonograms.

1)

2)

3)

4)

5)

28

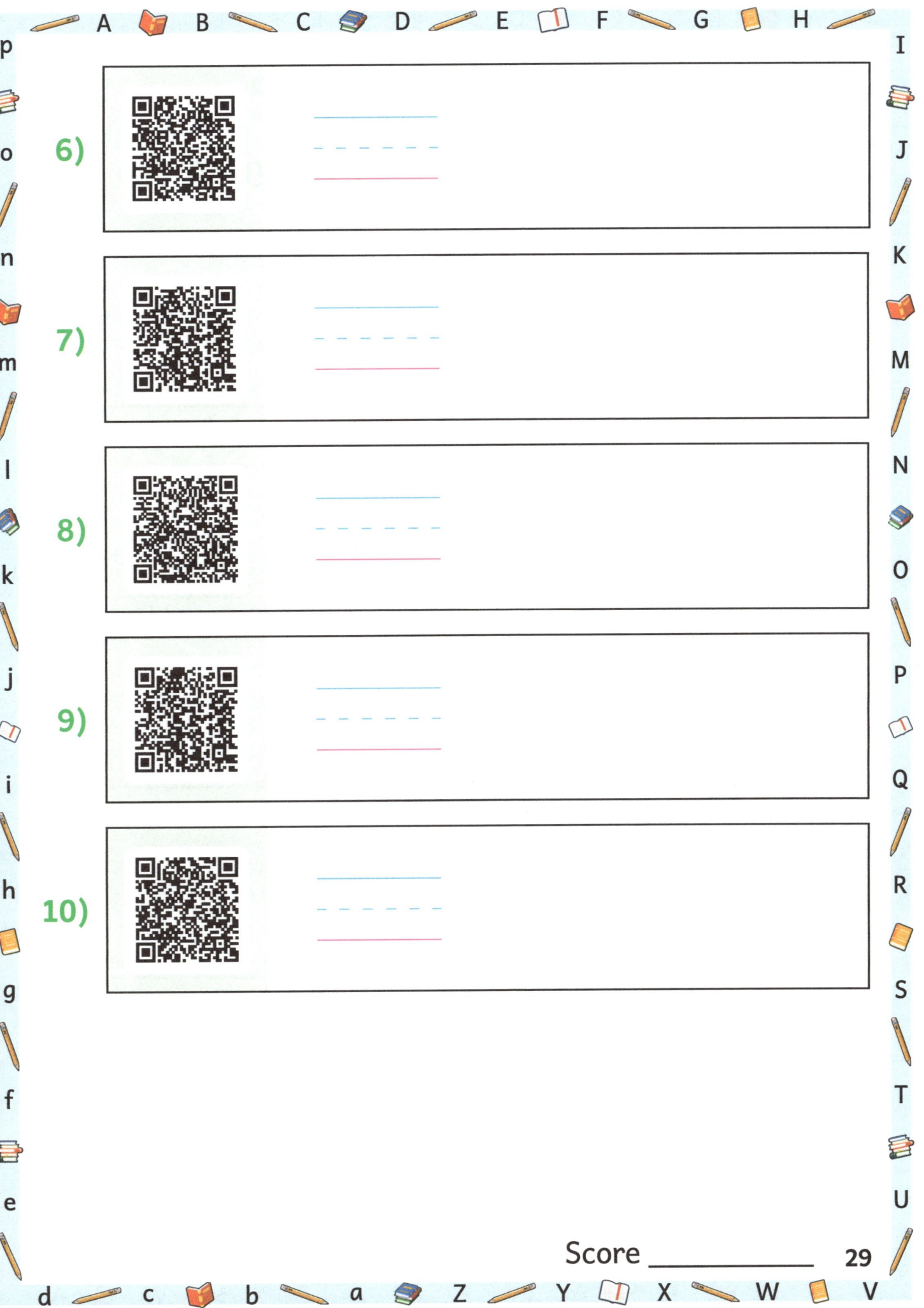

Spelling Test List 16

Listen to and write the spelling words.

1)

2)

3)

4)

5)

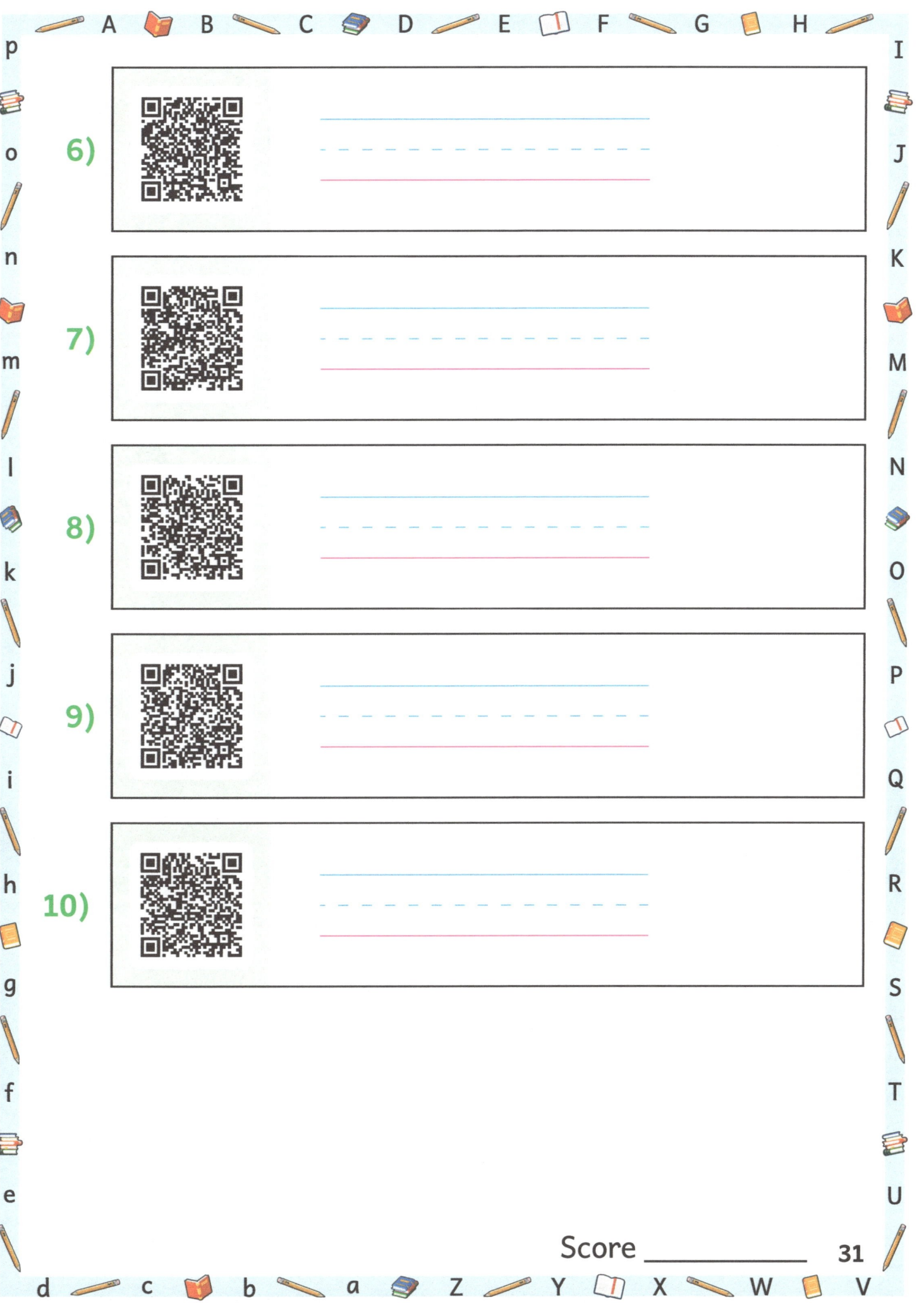

4. SPELLING LIST 17: Part 1

Learn:

- Write compound words.

- Spell and read words from List 17.

WRITING PHONOGRAM REVIEW

 **Listen to and write the phonograms.**
Underline any multi-letter phonograms.

WORKING WITH WORDS

The words in List 17 are compound words.

Spelling Rules

Compound Words: Do not change the spelling of a base word in a compound word.

horse + shoe = horseshoe

Match the pictures with the compound words.

1)

pitchfork

2)

dodgeball

3)

spaceship

4)

hometown

5)

racecar

Listen!

? Circle the correct answer.

6) | syllables | 1 2 3 4 |

? Circle the correct answers.
Then, write each part of the word.

7)
| base word | |
| sounds | 1 2 3 4 |

8)
| base word | |
| sounds | 1 2 3 4 |

 **Write and read.**

9)

Listen!

 **Circle the correct answer.**

10) | syllables | 1   2   3   4 |

 **Circle the correct answers.**
Then, write each part of the word.

11)
base word	
sounds	1 2 3 4

12)
base word	
sounds	1 2 3 4

 **Write and read.**

13)

Listen!

? **Circle the correct answer.**

14) | syllables | 1 2 3 4 |

? **Circle the correct answers.**
Then, write each part of the word.

15)
| base word | |
| sounds | 1 2 3 4 |

_____
- - - - - - - -
_____

16)
| base word | |
| sounds | 1 2 3 4 |

_____
- - - - - - - -
_____

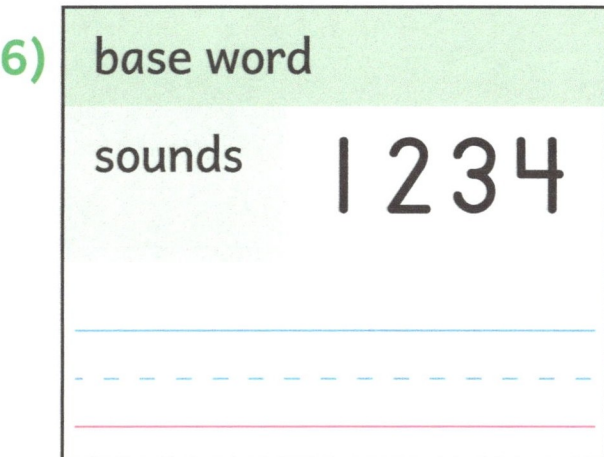 **Write and read.**

_____
- - - - - - - -
17) _____

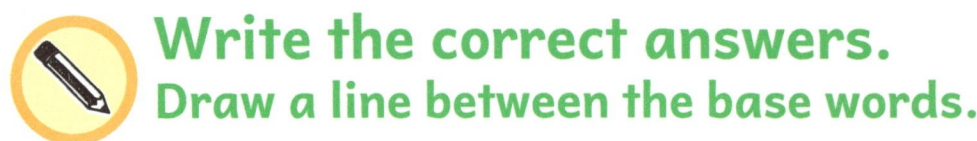

Write the correct answers.
Draw a line between the base words.

18) goodbye

19) backpack

20) outside

Write the correct answers.
Complete the sentences.

outside   goodbye   backpack

21) Kathleen put the books in her _____.

22) She said _____ to her teacher.

23) She went _____ to wait for her grandma.

SCORE   CORRECT   RESCORE

5. SPELLING LIST 17: Part 2

Learn:

- Identify compound words.

- Spell and read words from List 17.

WRITING PHONOGRAM REVIEW

✏️ **Listen to and write the phonograms.**
Underline any multi-letter phonograms.

WORKING WITH WORDS

Compound words are like puzzles. Two different words come together to mean something else.

+ = rainbow

Write the correct answers.
Make the compound words.

1)  + = _____

2)  + = _____

3)  + = _____

4)  + = _____

5)  + = _____

Listen!

? Circle the correct answer.

6) | syllables | 1 | 2 | 3 | 4 |

? Circle the correct answers.
Then, write each part of the word.

7) | base word |
| sounds | 1 2 3 4 |

_____
- - - - - - - - -
_____

8) | base word |
| sounds | 1 2 3 4 |

_____
- - - - - - - - -
_____

✏ Write and read.

_____
- - - - - - - - -
9) _____

Listen!

? **Circle the correct answer.**

10) | syllables | 1   2   3   4 |

? **Circle the correct answers.**
Then, write each part of the word.

11)
| base word | |
| sounds | 1 2 3 4 |

_____

- - - - - - -

_____

12)
| base word | |
| sounds | 1 2 3 4 |

_____

- - - - - - -

_____

 **Write and read.**

_____

- - - - - - -

13) _____

Listen!

? **Circle the correct answer.**

14) | syllables | 1   2   3   4 |

? **Circle the correct answers.**
Then, write each part of the word.

15)
base word
sounds   1 2 3 4

16)
base word
sounds   1 2 3 4

✏️ **Write and read.**

17) _____

Listen!

 **Circle the correct answer.**

18) | syllables | 1   2   3   4 |

 **Circle the correct answers.**
Then, write each part of the word.

19)

base word

sounds   1 2 3 4

_____

20)

base word

sounds   1 2 3 4

_____

Write and read.

21) _____

44

? Choose the correct answers.

22) Mark (☒) TWO words that have a VCe syllable.

☐ yourself   ☐ sidewalk   ☐ airplane

✏️ Write the correct answers.
Sort the words in ABC order.

| sidewalk | yourself | bedroom |

23) _____

24) _____

25) _____

✏️ Use the word in your own sentence.

| airplane |

26) _____

SCORE   CORRECT   RESCORE

6. SPELLING LIST 17: Part 3

Learn:

- Identify base words.

- Spell and read words from List 17.

WRITING PHONOGRAM REVIEW

 **Listen to and write the phonograms.**
Underline any multi-letter phonograms.

WORKING WITH WORDS

Many compound words share a base word.

Base Word: **ball**

ballpark   foot**ball**   base**ball**

 **Write the correct answers.**
Write the base word for each group.

1)   cupcake   pancake   cakewalk   _____

2)   wildfire   fireworks   firefly   _____

3)   steamboat   boatload   tugboat   _____

4)   pinwheel   wheelchair   cartwheel   _____

5)   houseboat   dollhouse   clubhouse   _____

Listen!

 **Circle the correct answer.**

6) | syllables | 1 2 3 4 |

 **Circle the correct answers.**
Then, write each part of the word.

7)
base word
sounds   1 2 3 4

8)
base word
sounds   1 2 3 4

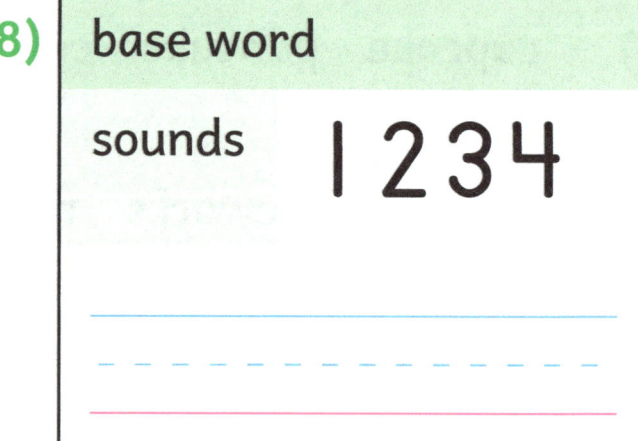 **Write and read.**

9)

48

Listen!

 **Circle the correct answer.**

10)
| syllables | 1 | 2 | 3 | 4 |

 **Circle the correct answers.**
Then, write each part of the word.

11)
| base word |
| sounds 1 2 3 4 |

12)
| base word |
| sounds 1 2 3 4 |

Write and read.

13)

Listen!

 **Circle the correct answer.**

14)	syllables	1	2	3	4

 **Circle the correct answers.**
Then, write each part of the word.

15)

base word

sounds	1 2 3 4

_____

16)

base word

sounds	1 2 3 4

_____

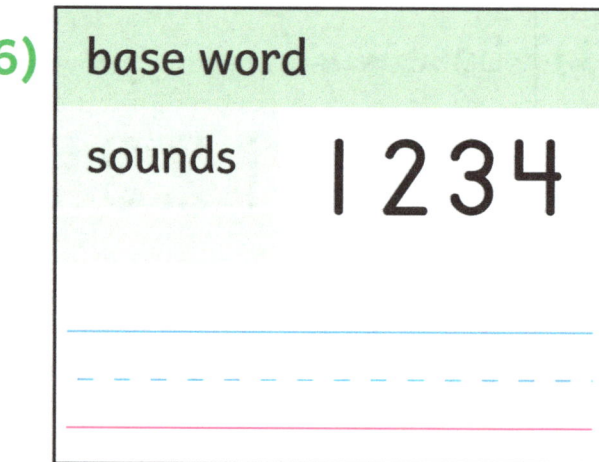 **Write and read.**

17) _____

 **Write the correct answers.**
Draw a line between the base words.

18) into

19) homework

 **Circle the correct answers.**
Which picture describes the sentence?

20) Jake put the flag on the **flagpole**.

21) Wesley left his **homework** on his bed.

22) A bird flew **into** our classroom.

SCORE   CORRECT   RESCORE

PHONOGRAM REVIEW

 Listen to and circle the correct phonograms.

1)    th   f   ph

2)    ui   oa   ou

3)    kn   ng   sh

4)    ey   er   wr

5)    d   v   th

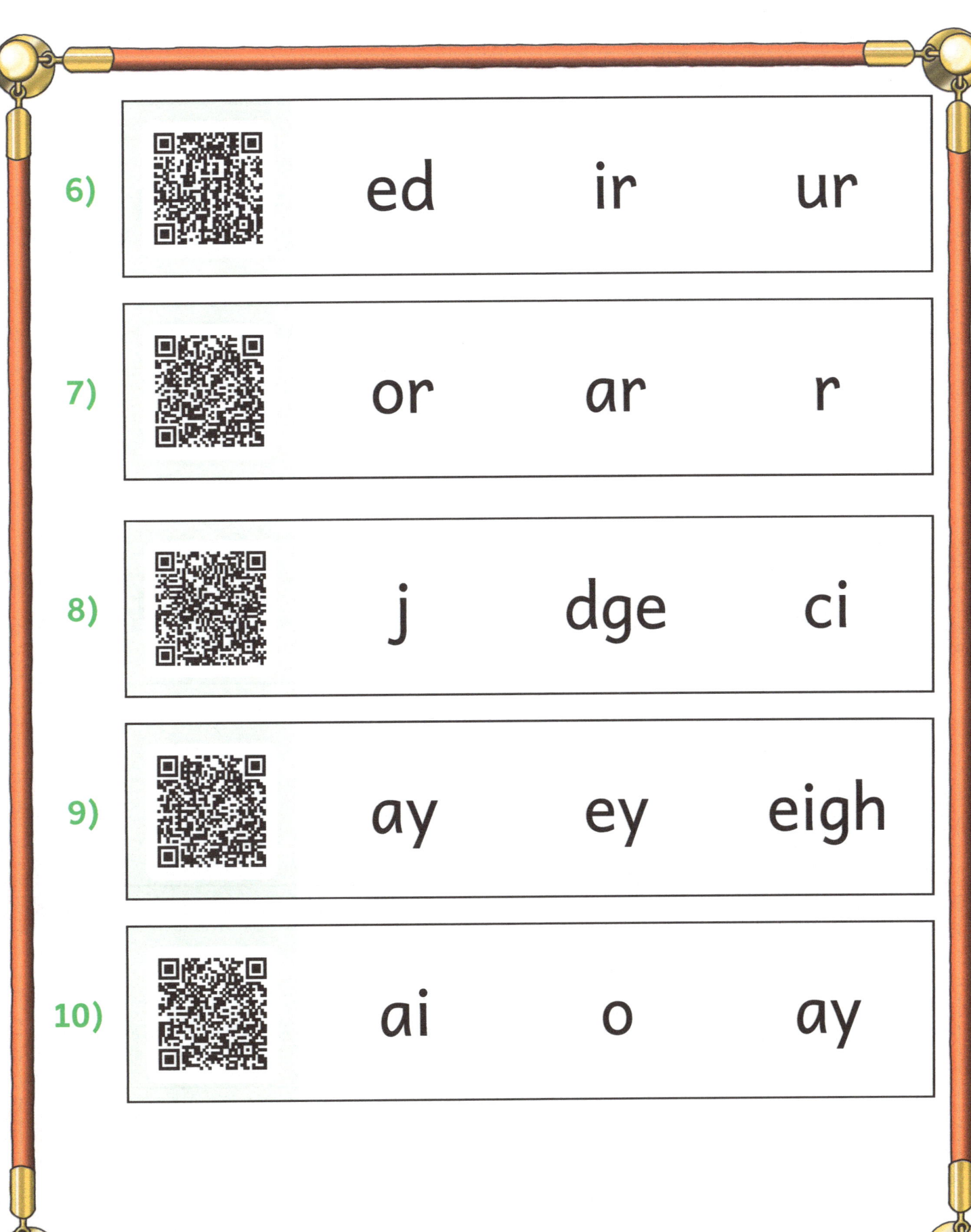

6)   ed   ir   ur

7)   or   ar   r

8)   j   dge   ci

9)   ay   ey   eigh

10)   ai   o   ay

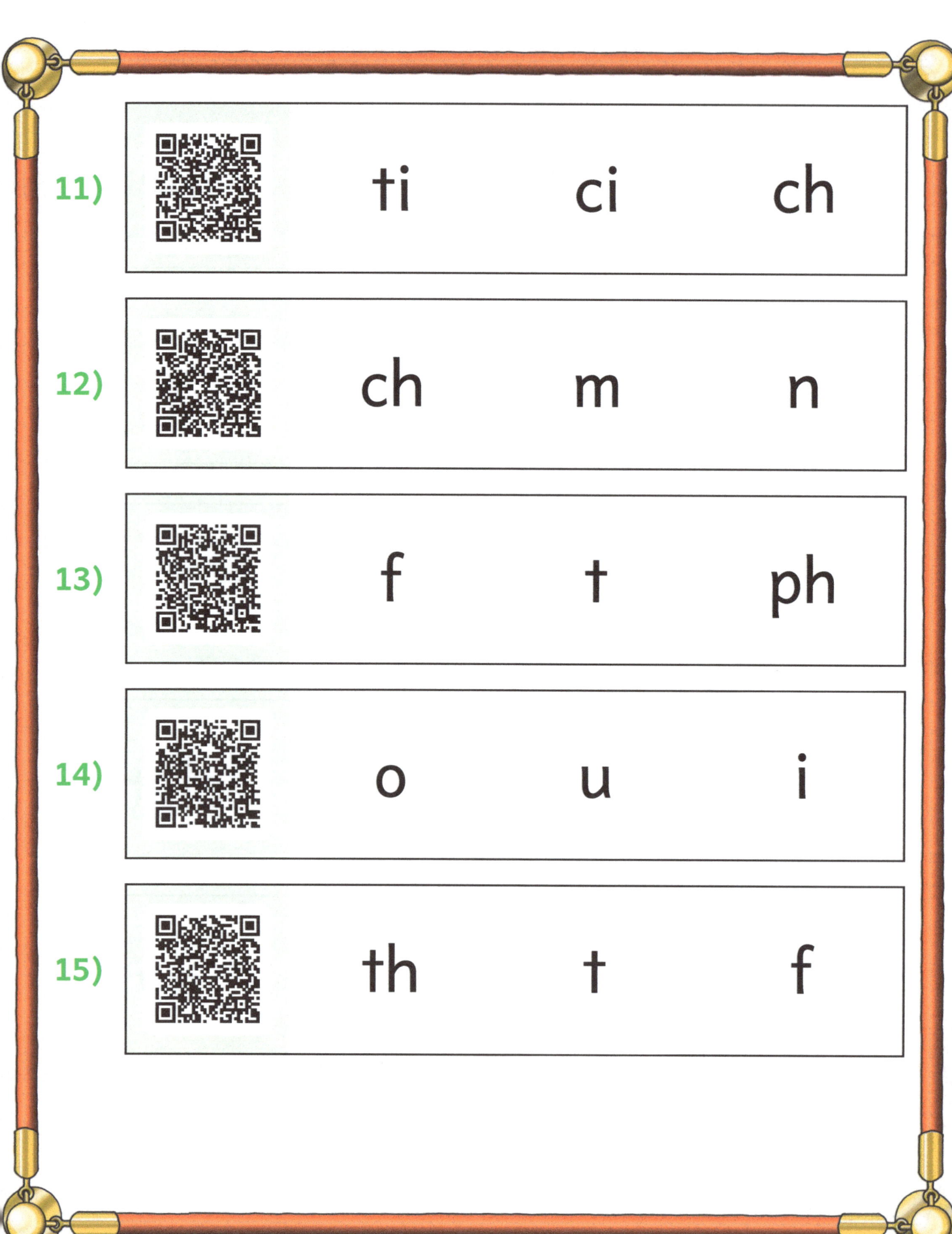

11) ti   ci   ch

12) ch   m   n

13) f   t   ph

14) o   u   i

15) th   t   f

54

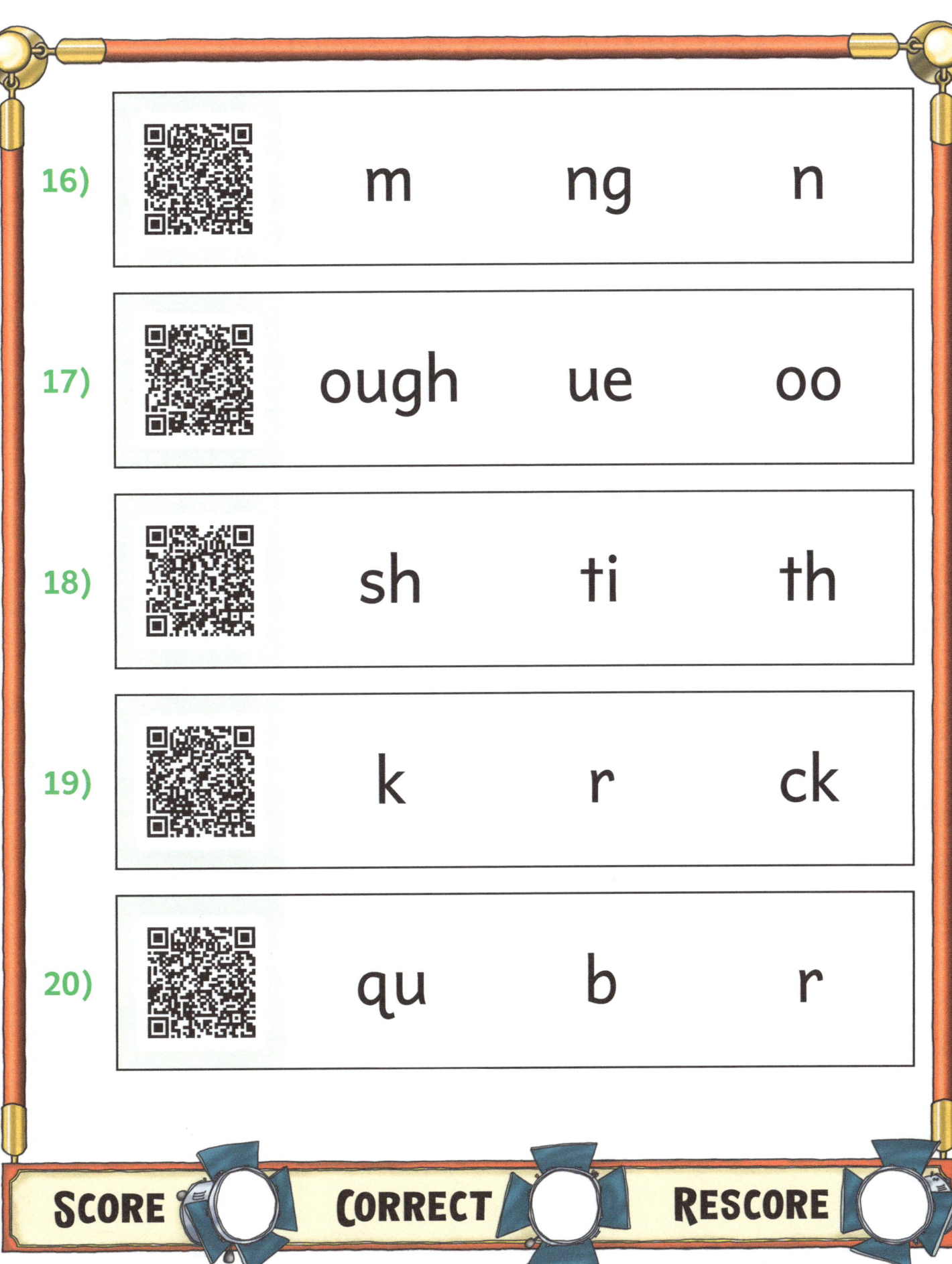

16) m   ng   n

17) ough   ue   oo

18) sh   ti   th

19) k   r   ck

20) qu   b   r

SCORE   CORRECT   RESCORE

SPELLING LIST 17 REVIEW

 **Write the correct answers.**
Sort the words in ABC order. You will need to use the second letter for some words.

into	outside	yourself
flagpole	airplane	goodbye
sidewalk	bedroom	homework
backpack		

1) _____

2) _____

3) _____

4) _____

5) _____

6) _____

7) _____

8) _____

9) _____

10) _____

This Reader has the tricky word *hour*.
The letter **h** is silent.

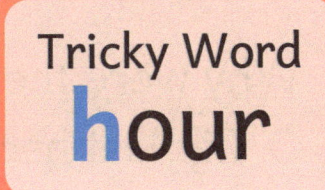

Tricky Word
hour

Write the correct answers.
Complete the sentences.

howling	lunch	walk

1) The hungry hippos have one hour to eat _____.

2) It takes Henry less than an hour to _____ home.

3) Holly's hound spent two hours _____ at the moon.

Time to
Read!

Reader 24

The Homework
Hunt

 **Choose the correct answers.**

4) Why were the pals looking for things?
   ○ Zip lost her homework.
   ○ It was their homework.
   ○ They were working for the lost and found.

5) How many things did each pal need to find?
   ○ 1
   ○ 5
   ○ 2

6) What did the pals have to do when they found something?
   ○ take a photo with it
   ○ put it in their backpack
   ○ mark it with a sticker

Phonogram Test 29

Listen to and write the correct phonograms.
Underline any multi-letter phonograms.

1)

2)

3)

4)

5)

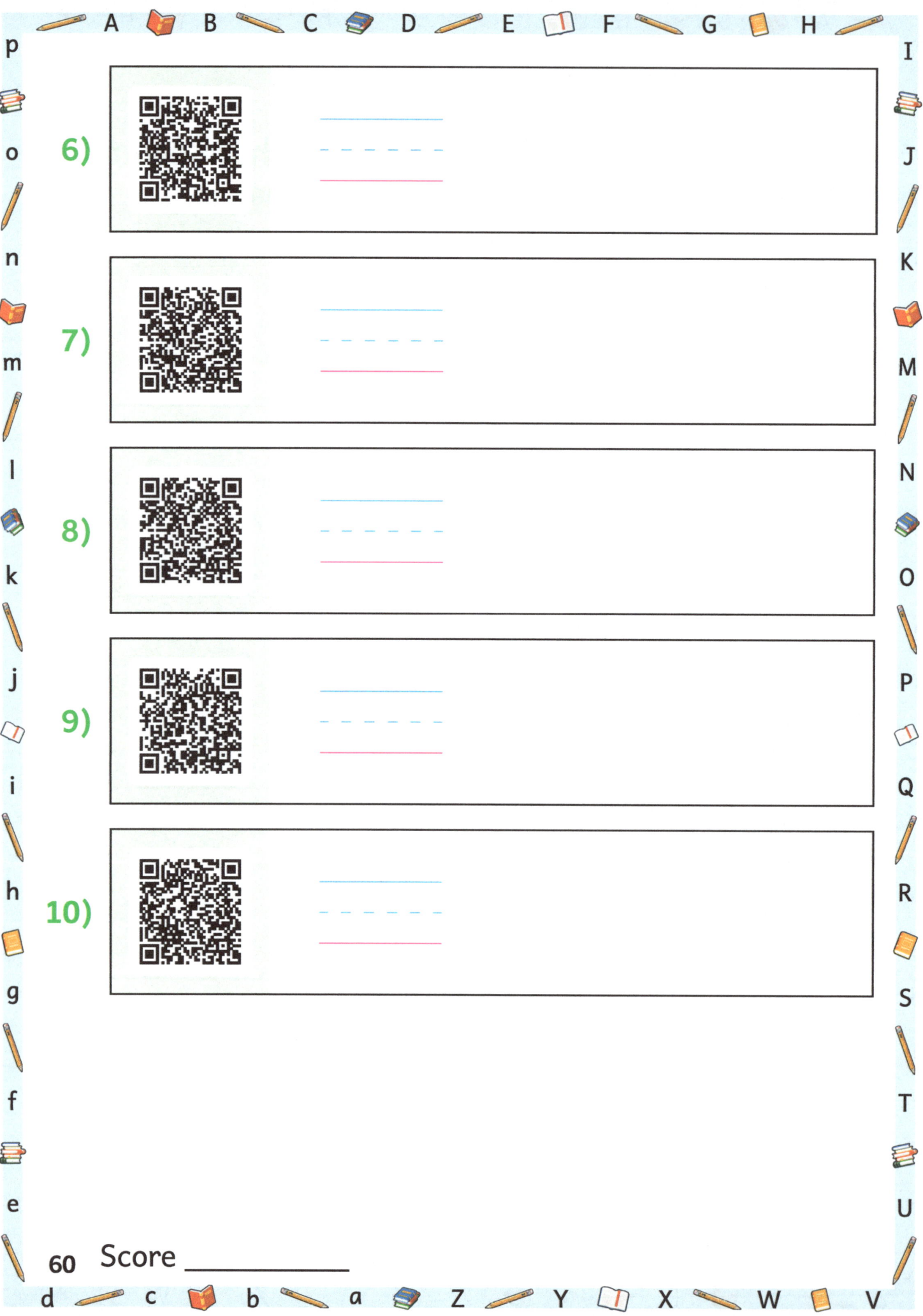

A B C D E F G H I J K L M N O P Q R S T U V W X Y Z a b c d e f g h i j k l m n o p

6)

7)

8)

9)

10)

60 Score _____

Spelling Test List 17

Listen to and write the spelling words.

1)

2)

3)

4)

5)

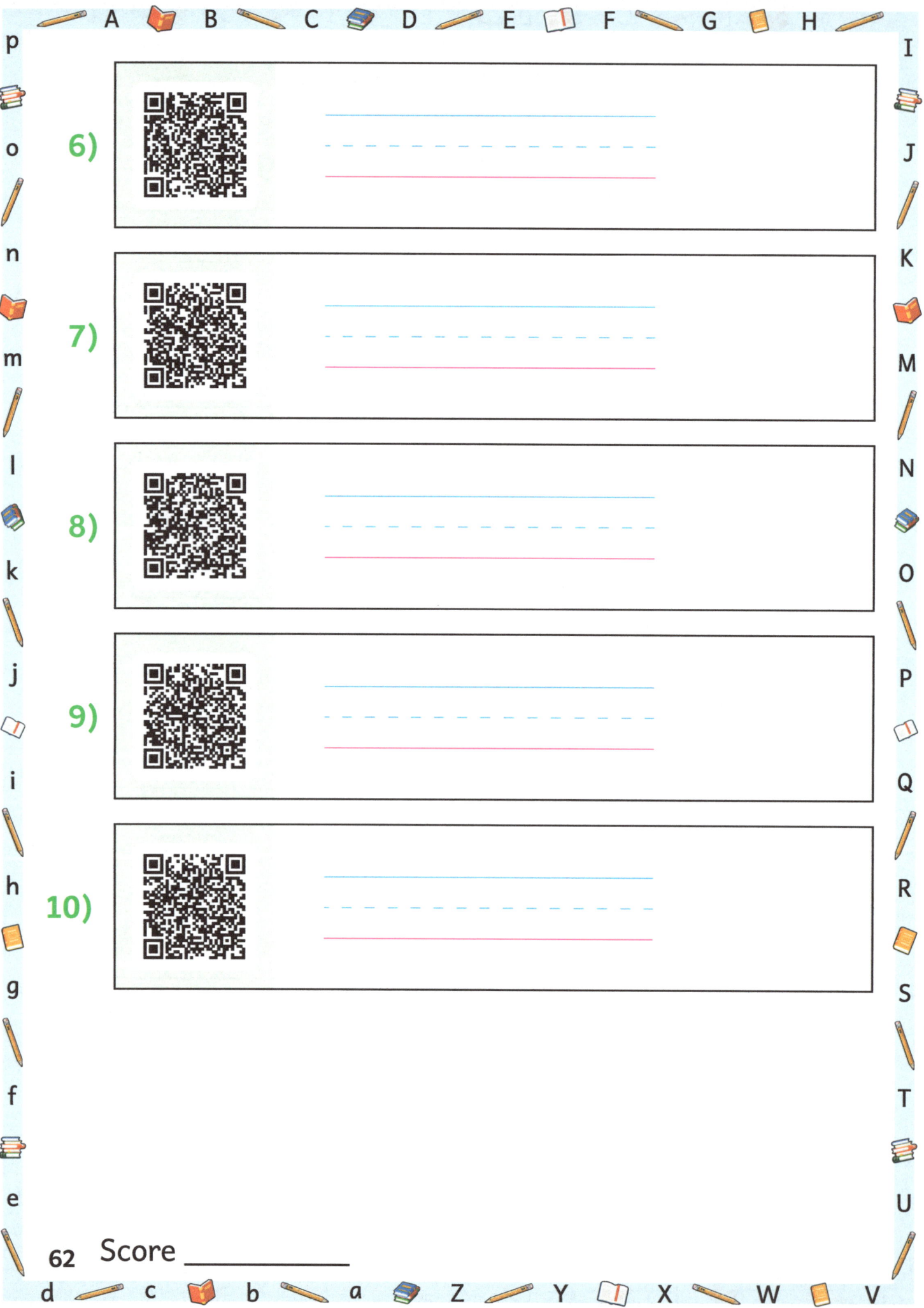

6)

7)

8)

9)

10)

Score _____

7. SPELLING LIST 18: Part 1

Learn:

- Count syllables in written words.

- Spell and read words from List 18.

WRITING PHONOGRAM REVIEW

✏️ **Listen to and write the phonograms.**
Underline any multi-letter phonograms.

WORKING WITH WORDS

This Lesson has words with vowel team **igh**. It makes the long **i** sound.

Write the correct answers.
Circle the vowel sounds. Then, write the number of syllables.

1) twilight _____

2) fright _____

3) mighty _____

4) delight _____

5) sigh _____

 Circle the correct answers.

6)	syllables	1	2	3	4

7)	sounds	1	2	3	4

 Write and read.

8) _____

 Choose the correct answer.

9) What is the syllable type?
- ○ vowel team
- ○ open
- ○ r-controlled

Listen!

 **Circle the correct answers.**

10)	syllables	1	2	3	4

11)	sounds	1	2	3	4

 **Write and read.**

12) _____

 **Choose the correct answer.**

13) The vowel sound is ____.
- ○ short
- ○ r-controlled
- ○ long

Listen!

 **Circle the correct answers.**

14)	syllables	1	2	3	4

15)	sounds	1	2	3	4

 **Write and read.**

16) _____

 **Choose the correct answer.**

17) Which position is the vowel in?
- ○ beginning
- ○ middle
- ○ ending

Choose the correct answer.

18) Which word begins with two consonant sounds?

    ○ bright   ○ might   ○ light

Write the correct answers.
Complete the sentences.

bright	light	might

19) Tonight, we _____ get to see the space station.

20) It reflects the _____ from the sun.

21) It will look like a _____ star flying in the sky.

8. SPELLING LIST 18: Part 2

Learn:

- Read sentences with vowel teams **oo** and **ow**.

- Spell and read words from List 18.

WRITING PHONOGRAM REVIEW

Listen to and write the phonograms.
Underline any multi-letter phonograms.

WORKING WITH WORDS

This Lesson has the vowel teams **oo** and **ow**.

? **Read the sentences.**
Underline the word for the missing item in each picture. Then, color the missing item.

1) The goose has a crown.

2) The raccoon has a balloon.

3) The owl has a flower.

4) The rooster has a pillow.

Listen!

? **Circle the correct answers.**

| 5) | syllables | 1 | 2 | 3 | 4 |

| 6) | sounds | 1 | 2 | 3 | 4 |

✏️ **Write and read.**

7) _____

? **Choose the correct answer.**

8) What is the syllable type?

　○ open

　○ r-controlled

　○ vowel team

Listen!

 **Circle the correct answers.**

9)	syllables	1	2	3	4

10)	sounds	1	2	3	4

 **Write and read.**

11) _____

 **Choose the correct answer.**

12) The vowel makes its ____ sound.
- ○ first
- ○ second
- ○ third

Listen!

 **Circle the correct answers.**

| 13) | syllables | 1 | 2 | 3 | 4 |

| 14) | sounds | 1 | 2 | 3 | 4 |

 **Write and read.**

15) _____

 **Choose the correct answer.**

16) The vowel makes its ____ sound.
   ○ first
   ○ second
   ○ third

Listen!

 **Circle the correct answers.**

17)	syllables	1	2	3	4

18)	sounds	1	2	3	4

 **Write and read.**

19) _____

 **Choose the correct answer.**

20) Which reading rule does this word follow?
   ○ **o** before **m**, **n**, or **v**
   ○ 2nd sound of **c**
   ○ 1st sound of **c**

 **Choose the correct answer.**

21) How are these four spelling words the same?

broom   snow   clown   crown

   O   The have the same vowel team.

   O   They have the same vowel sound.

   O   They begin with two consonant sounds.

 **Write the correct answers.**
Sort the words in ABC order.

clown   crowd   broom

22) _____   **23)** _____   **24)** _____

 **Use the word in your own sentence.**

snow

25) _____

SCORE   CORRECT   RESCORE

Learn:

- Divide and read two-syllable words.

- Spell and read words from List 18.

WRITING PHONOGRAM REVIEW

✏️ **Listen to and write the phonograms.**
Underline any multi-letter phonograms.

WORKING WITH WORDS

This Lesson has words with vowel team **ai**. It is not used at the end of words like vowel team **ay**.

v c | c v
s u s | t <u>ai</u> n
Closed   Vowel Team

v | c v
r e | l <u>ay</u>
Open   Vowel Team

Mark, divide, and read the words.
Remember, underline the multi-letter phonograms first.

parlay

raisin

subway

railroad

delay

trailer

remain

77

Listen!

 **Circle the correct answers.**

1)	syllables	1	2	3	4

2)	sounds	1	2	3	4

 **Write and read.**

3) _____

 **Choose the correct answer.**

4) What is the syllable type?
   - ○ vowel team
   - ○ open
   - ○ VCe

Listen!

 **Circle the correct answers.**

5)	syllables	1	2	3	4

6)	sounds	1	2	3	4

 **Write and read.**

7) _____

 **Choose the correct answer.**

8) Which reading rule does this word follow?
- ○ 3rd sound of **a**
- ○ beginning **s**
- ○ 1st sound of **c**

Listen!

 **Circle the correct answers.**

| 9) | syllables | 1 | 2 | 3 | 4 |

| 10) | sounds | 1 | 2 | 3 | 4 |

 **Write and read.**

11) _____

 **Choose the correct answer.**

12) The vowel sound is ____.
   ○ long
   ○ short
   ○ r-controlled

80

 # Choose the correct answers.

13) Mark (☒) TWO words that rhyme.

☐ snail   ☐ brain   ☐ train

Circle the correct answers.
Which picture describes the sentence?

14) I like to ride the **train**.

15) The **snail** has a blue shell.

16) Our teacher showed us a fake **brain**.

SCORE   CORRECT   RESCORE

PHONOGRAM REVIEW

 Listen to and circle the correct phonograms.

1)  wr   gn   th

2)  oy   ow   ou

3)  ee   y   ie

4)  wor   ough   au

5)  c   d   ci

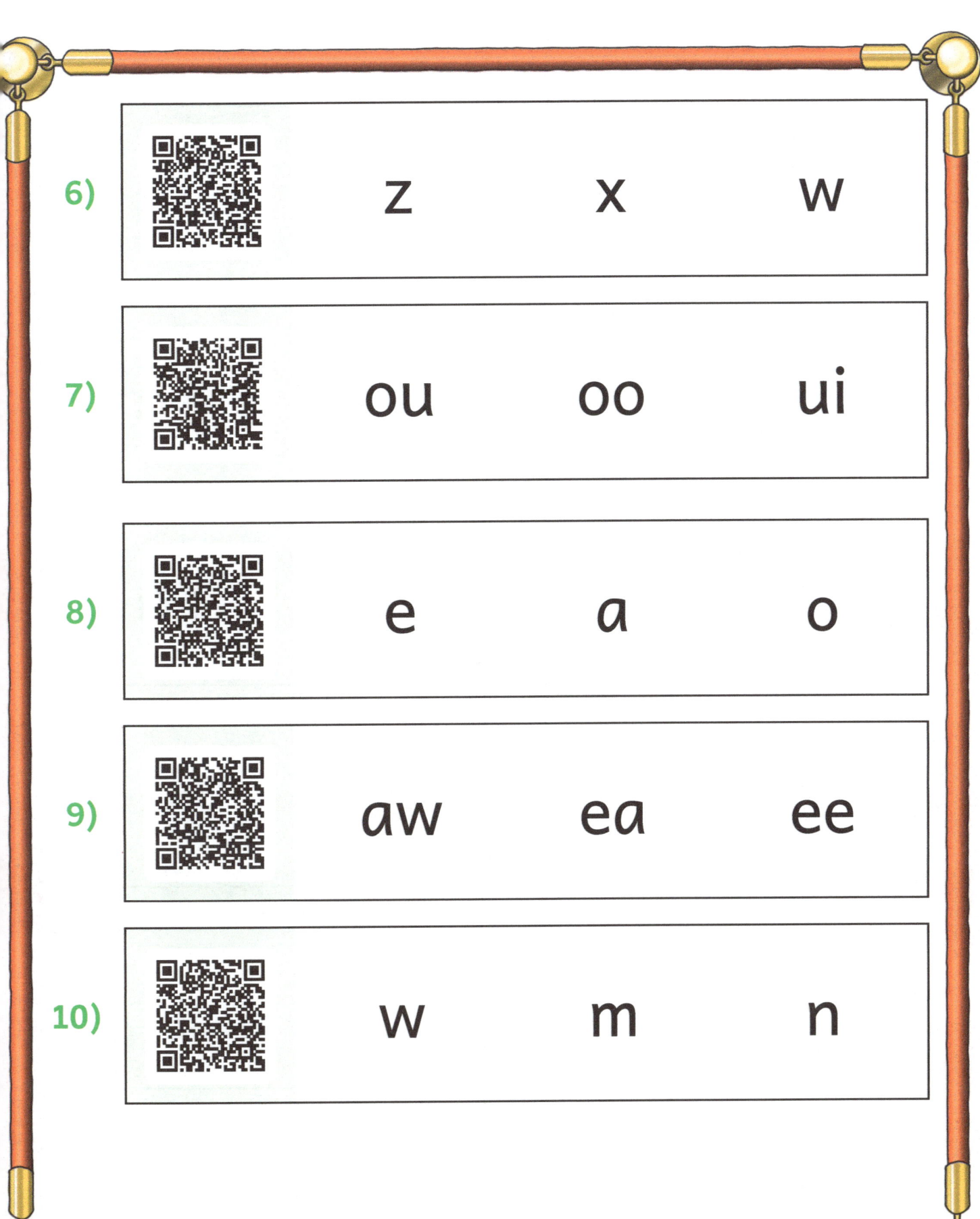

6)   z   x   w

7)   ou   oo   ui

8)   e   a   o

9)   aw   ea   ee

10)   w   m   n

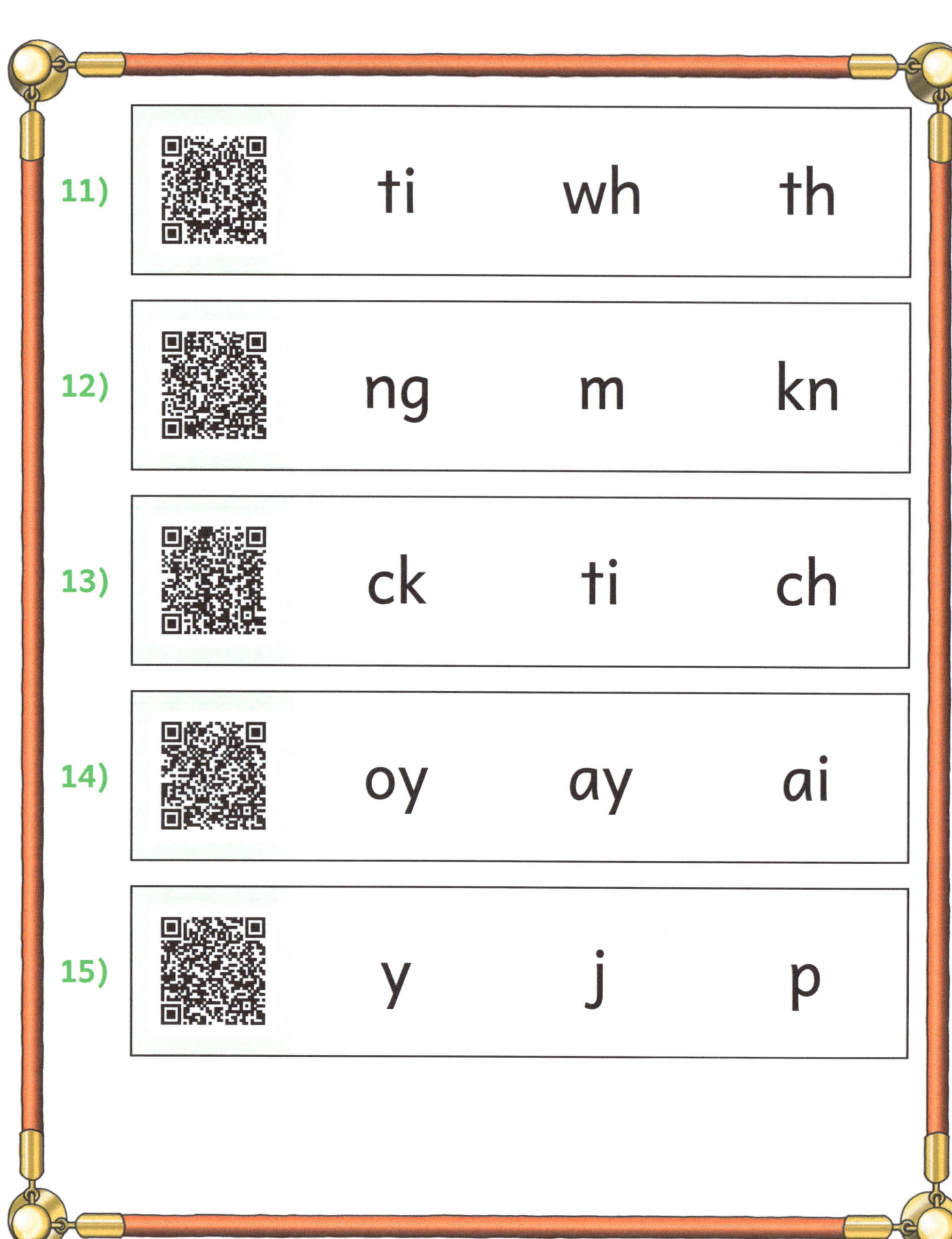

11) ti   wh   th

12) ng   m   kn

13) ck   ti   ch

14) oy   ay   ai

15) y   j   p

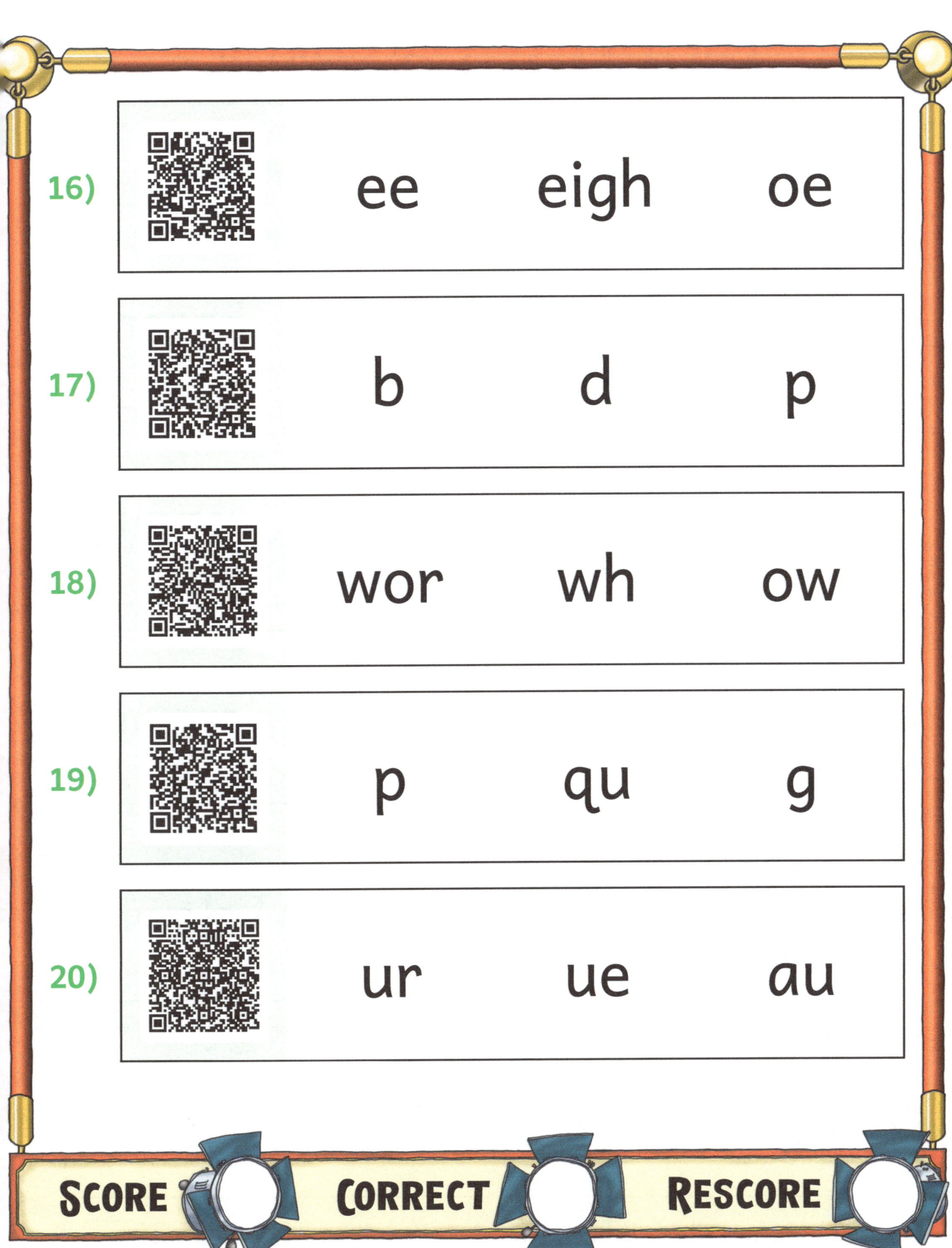

16) ee   eigh   oe

17) b   d   p

18) wor   wh   ow

19) p   qu   g

20) ur   ue   au

SCORE   CORRECT   RESCORE

SPELLING LIST 18 REVIEW

 **Listen to and circle the correct words.**

1)  brain   bright   broom

2)  crowd   clown   snail

3)  snail   snow   crowd

4)  crowd   broom   clown

5)  train   snow   snail

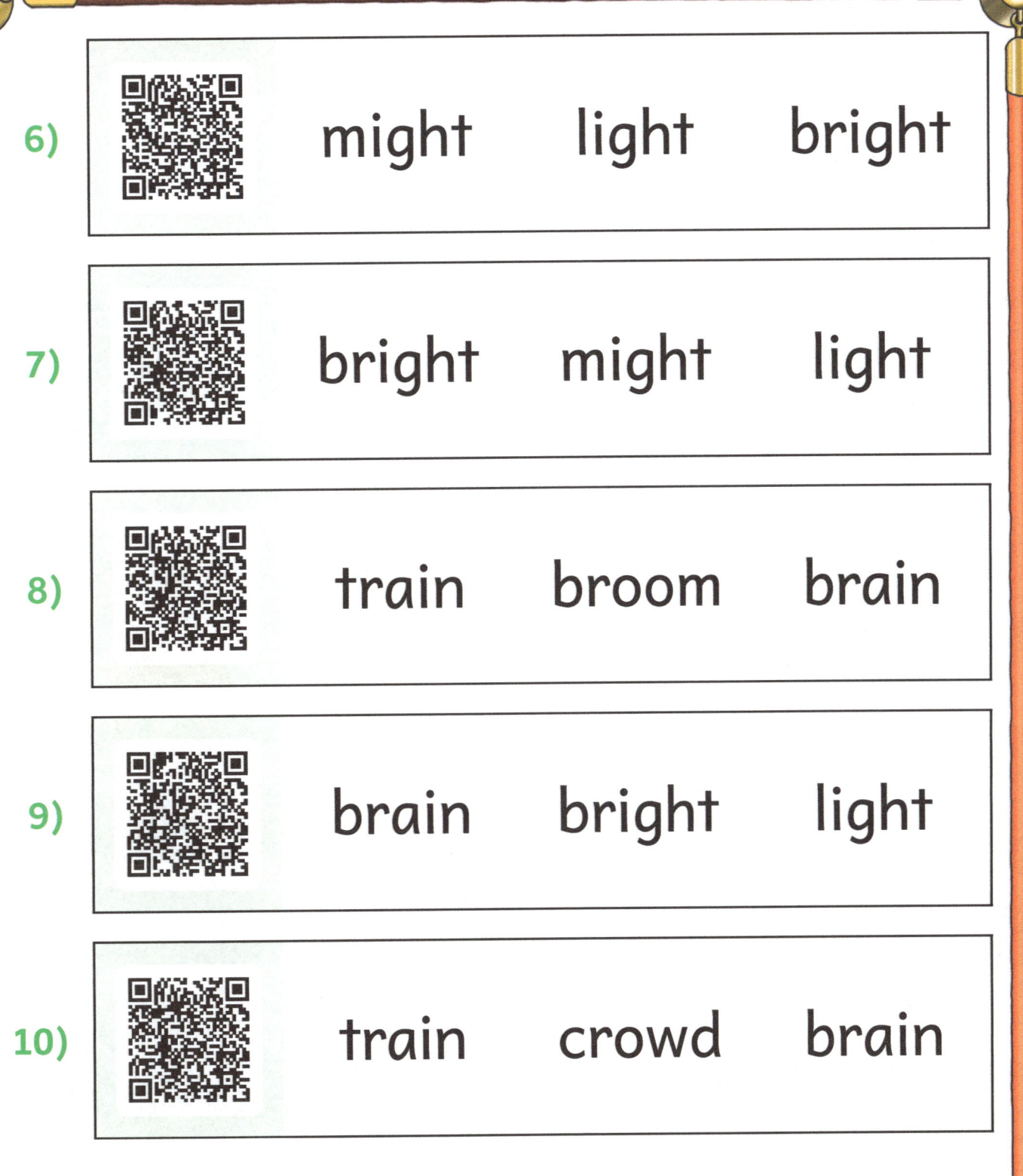

6)   might   light   bright

7)   bright   might   light

8)   train   broom   brain

9)   brain   bright   light

10)   train   crowd   brain

READER 25: "The Big Train Ride"

Before you read, practice these words.

 **Read and trace the words.**

1) through

2) mountains

3) sunshine

4) ready

5) thunder

6) lightning

Reader 25

The Big Train Ride

? Choose the correct answers.

7) What did the pals see in the first town?

- ○ a circus
- ○ a mailbox
- ○ a snail

8) Why was Pip worried?

- ○ He left something back on the beach.
- ○ He did not like how tall the mountains were.
- ○ He thought the train was going too fast.

9) What was the last train stop?

- ○ the mountains
- ○ a new town
- ○ a lunch break

Phonogram Test 30

Listen to and write the correct phonograms.
Underline any multi-letter phonograms.

1)

2)

3)

4)

5)

90

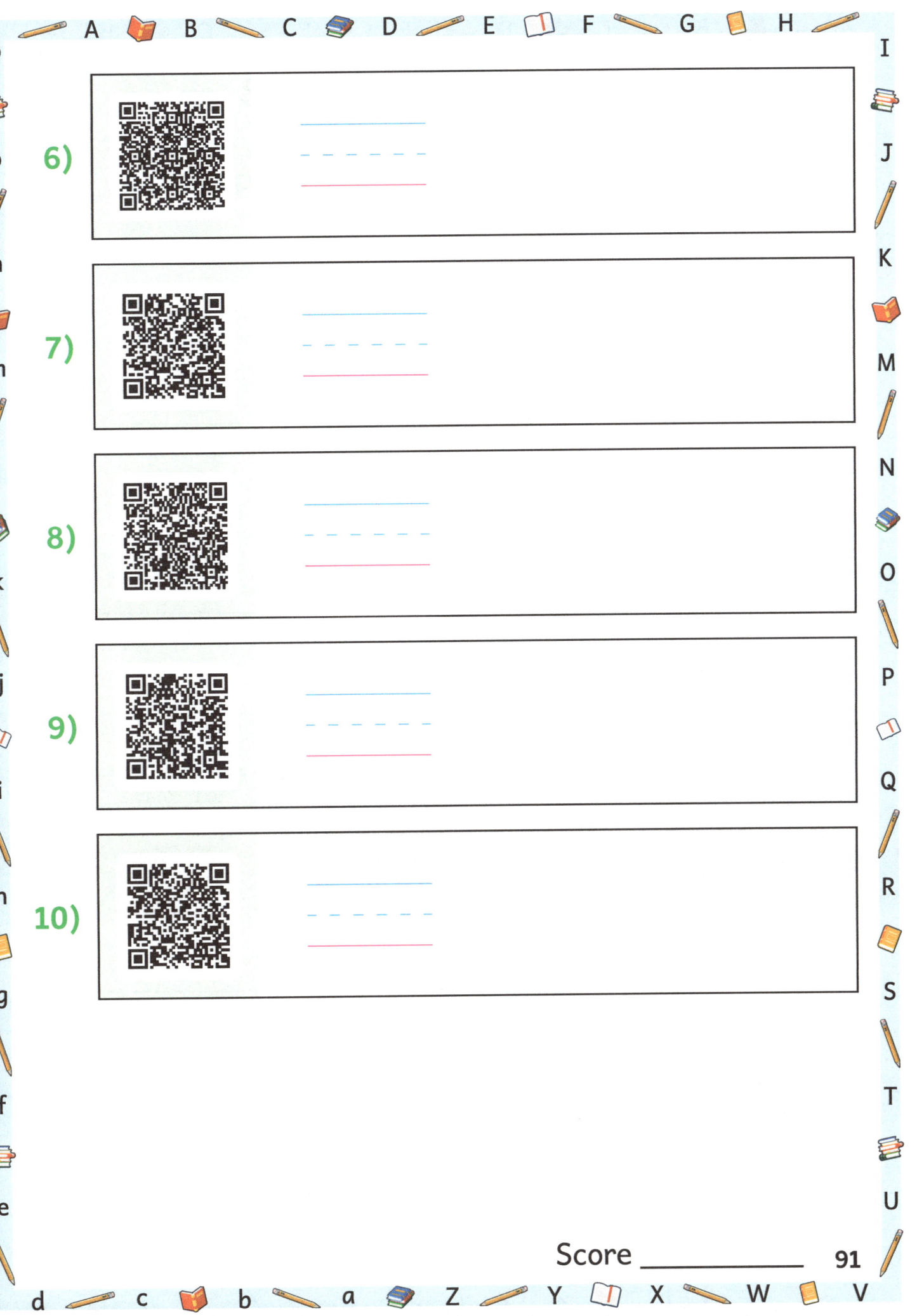

Spelling Test List 18

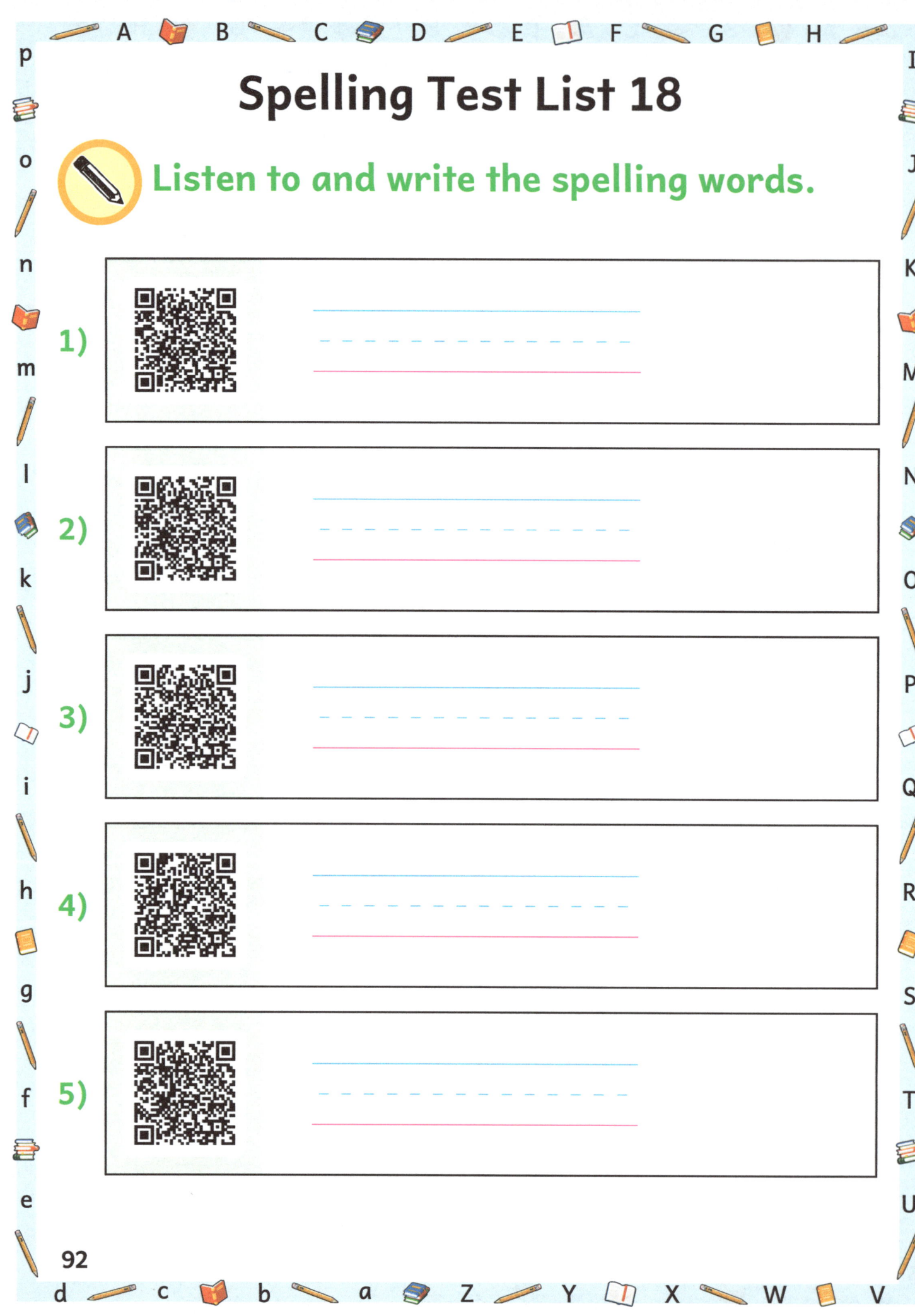

Listen to and write the spelling words.

1)

2)

3)

4)

5)

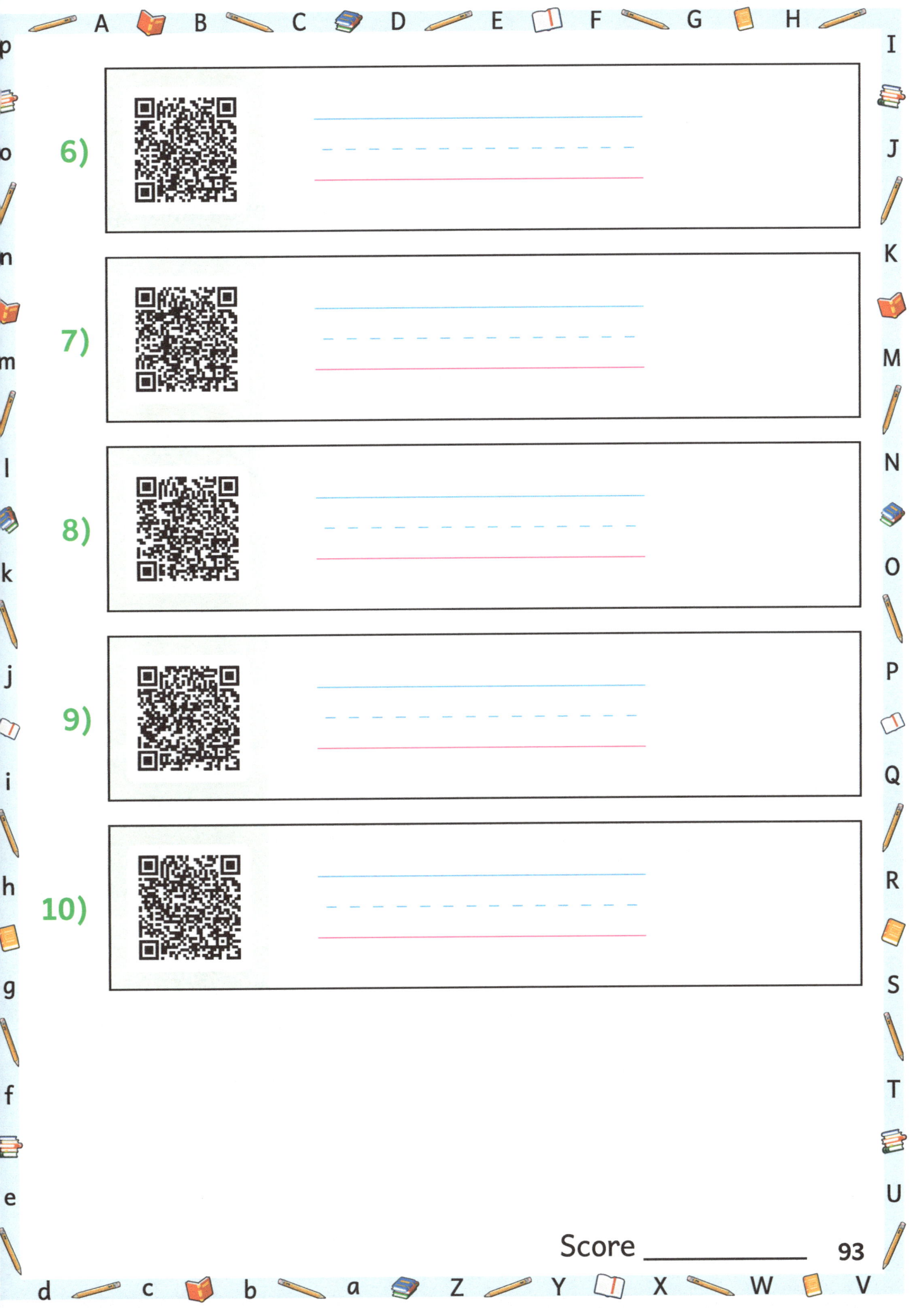

6)

7)

8)

9)

10)

PAPERCRAFT: Oat

To Do:

For best results, fold then unfold lines before building.

 **Head**

- Fold into a box shape.
- Secure tabs with glue.

 **Body**

- Fold into a box shape.
- Secure tabs with glue.

 **Build**

- Attach head to body with glue.